Reading Comprehension

Table of Contents

Glossary 2
Main Idea 3
Comprehension 4
Comprehension 5
Recognizing Details 6
Comprehension 7
Recognizing Details 8
Review 9
Sequencing 10
Comprehension 11
Following Directions 12
Comprehension 13
Context 14
Comprehension 15
Context 16
Review 17
Comprehension 18
Context 19
Comprehension 20
Fact or Opinion? 21
Comprehension 22
Fact or Opinion? 23
Review 24
Following Directions 25
Comprehension 26
Sequencing 27
Comprehension 28
Main Idea 29
Comprehension 30
Recognizing Details 31
Review 32

Copyright © 1994 American Education Publishing Co.

Reading Comprehension

Glossary

Comprehension. Understanding what is seen, heard or read.

Context. A way to figure out the meaning of a new word by relating it to the other words in the sentence.

Fact or Opinion. A fact can be proved. An opinion, which cannot be proved, tells what someone believes.

Following Directions. Doing what the directions say to do.

Main Idea. Finding the most important points.

Recognizing Details. Being able to pick out and remember the who, what, when, where, why and how of what is read.

Sequencing. Putting things in order.

Reading Comprehension

Name: _____

Main Idea: Where Did Songs Come From?

Historians say the earliest music was probably connected to religion. Long ago, people believed the world was controlled by a variety of gods. Keeping the gods happy was believed to be very important to survival. Singing was among the first things humans did to show respect to the gods.

Singing is still an important part of most religions. Buddhists (bood-ists), Christians and Jews all use chants and/or songs in their religious ceremonies. The Christian Bible instructs those who love God to "make a joyful noise unto the Lord …" and other religions provide similar instructions. If you have ever sung a song — religious or otherwise — you know that singing is fun. The feeling of joy that comes from singing must also have made ancient people feel happy.

Another time people sang was when they worked. Sailors sang as they pulled heavy ropes. Slaves sang as they carried the heavy stones to build the pyramids. Soldiers sang as they marched into battle. Farmers sang one song as they planted and another when they harvested. Singing made the work less burdensome. People used the tunes to pace themselves. Sometimes they followed instructions through songs.

For example, "Yo-oh, heave, ho!/Yo-oh, heave, ho!" was sung when sailors pulled in a ship's heavy ropes. "Heave" means to throw and that is what they did with the ropes as the sang the song. The song helped sailors work together and pull at the same time. This made the task easier.

Directions: Answer these questions about music.

1. The main idea is:

    Singing is fun and that is why early people liked it so much.

    Singing began as a way to show respect to the gods and is still an important part of most religious ceremonies.

2. Besides religious ceremonies, what other activity fostered singing?

   _____

3. What two types of songs did farmers sing? _____

4. How did singing "Yo-oh, heave ho!" help sailors work? _____

Comprehension: Facts About Folk Music

Folk music literally means "of the folks," and it belongs to everyone. The names of writers of folk music like Woody Guthrie and Pete Seeger are well-known among people over the age of 35. But the names of the musicians who composed most folk music have long been forgotten.

Folk music has remained popular because it tells about the lives of people. Usually, the tune and words are simple and easy to remember. Do you know the words to "She'll Be Comin' 'Round the Mountain"? Like other folk songs, it has many verses.

Although no one ever says who "she" is, the verses tell you that she will be riding six white horses and that "we'll all go out to greet her". The song's many verses also describe what will be eaten when she comes (chicken and dumplings) and what those singing will be wearing (red pajamas). Like many other folk songs, "She'll Be Comin' 'Round the Mountain" is a cheerful, rollicking song.

Not all folk songs are cheerful, however. Do you know the words to "Clementine"? "Clementine" came out of the California goldrush in the mid-1800s. It tells the story of "My darling, who's lost and gone forever," when Clementine was killed in a mine cave-in. ("In a cavern, in a canyon, excavating for a mine/Met a miner '49er and his darling, Clementine".)

Another famous fold song is "Swing Low, Sweet Chariot". This song was sung by slaves in the United States, and today is sung by people of all races. The chariot (charry-ut) is the chariot of God. The words, "Swing low, sweet chariot, coming for to carry me home…" describe the soul being united with God after death. Like other folk songs that sprang from slaves, "Swing Low, Sweet Chariot" is simple, moving and powerful.

Directions: Answer these questions about folk music.

1. Do people usually know who composed popular folk music? _____

2. Name two modern composers of folk music.

_____

3. What food is sung about in "She'll Be Comin' 'Round the Mountain"?

_____

4. Where did Clementine live?

   ☐ Florida   ☐ Mississippi   ☐ California

5. Clementine was killed in a

   ☐ mountain   ☐ mine   ☐ river

Reading Comprehension  Name: _____

Comprehension: Jazz Notes

Jazz, which began in the southern United States, became popular in the late 1800's. Like some folk songs, jazz was the music made by African-American people. It was the music of former slaves.

The rhythm and the beat of early jazz reflected the roots of black Americans in Africa. Many early jazz musicians could not read music. They sometimes made up their music as they went along on their clarinets, trumpets and other instruments. This "on the spot composing" is called "improvising". Modern jazz musicians carry on this tradition of improvising.

To improvise, a musician's grasp of music must go far beyond technical understanding. A jazz musician really must put a little of his own heart into what he plays. If you have ever seen jazz musicians at work, you know that the effort and joy they put into their music is enormous. Two of the most famous jazz musicians are trumpet players Louis Armstrong and Miles Davis.

Jazz music is often upbeat. It reflects the musicians' joy in living. Have you ever heard the expression, "Let's jazz this up"? To "jazz up" means to make something livelier. Even if you have never heard jazz played, you can imagine that it is anything but dreary!

Four to ten musicians usually make up a jazz band. Besides the trumpet and clarinet, a jazz band may include drums, piano, bass guitar, and sometimes a saxophone, violin and flute.

Directions: Answer these questions about jazz music.

1. Why did early jazz musicians improvise?

_____

2. What does "improvise" mean?

_____

3. Name two famous jazz musicians.

_____

4. Jazz music is

☐ slow   ☐ upbeat   ☐ dreary

5. Which of the following is not a jazz instrument?

☐ drum   ☐ piano   ☐ organ   ☐ violin   ☐ flute

Reading Comprehension   Name: _____

Recognizing Details: Flutes, Oboes, Clarinets, Bassoons

There are four kinds of woodwind instruments in modern bands. They are flutes, oboes, clarinets and bassoons. They are called "woodwind" instruments for two sensible reasons. In the beginning, they were all made of wood. Also, the musician's breath, or "wind" was required to play them.

Although they are all woodwinds, these instruments look different and are played differently. To play an oboe, the musician blows through a mouthpiece on the front of the instrument. The mouthpiece, called a "reed," is made of two flat pieces of a kind of wood called cane. Clarinet players also blow into a reed mouthpiece. The clarinet has only one reed in its mouthpiece.

To play the flute, the musician blows across the hole. The way the breath is aimed helps to make the flute's different sounds. The bassoon is the largest woodwind instrument. Bassoon players blow through a mouthpiece that goes through a short metal pipe before it goes into the body of the bassoon. It makes a very different sound from the clarinet or the oboe.

Woodwind instruments also have keys — but not the kind of keys that open locks. These keys are more like levers that the musician pushes up and down. The levers cover holes. When the musician pushes down on the lever, it closes that hole. When she lifts her finger, it opens the hole. Different sounds are produced by controlling the amount of breath, or "wind," that goes through the holes.

Directions: Answer these questions about woodwind instruments.

1. What instruments are in the woodwind section?

_____

2. Why are some instruments called woodwinds?

_____

3. How is a flute different from the other woodwinds?

_____

4. When a musician pushes down on a woodwind key, what happens?

_____

5. How would a woodwind musician open the holes on her instrument?

_____

Comprehension: Harp Happenings

If you have ever heard a harpist play, you know what a lovely sound a harp makes. Music experts say the harp is among the oldest of instruments. It probably was invented several thousand years ago in or near Egypt.

The first harps are believed to have been made by stretching a string tightly between an empty tortoise shell and a curved pole. The empty shell magnified the sound the string made when it was plucked. More strings were added later so that more sounds could be made. Over the centuries, the shape of the harp gradually was changed into that of the large, graceful instruments we recognize today.

Here is how a harpist plays a harp. She leans the harp against her right shoulder. She puts her hands on either side of the harp and plucks its strings with both hands. A harp has seven pedals on the bottom back. The audience usually cannot see these pedals. Most people are surprised to learn about them.

The pedals are connected to the strings. Stepping on a particular pedal causes certain strings to tighten. The tightening and loosening of the strings makes different sounds. So does the way the strings are plucked with the hands.

At first glance, harps look like simple instruments. Actually, they are rather complicated and difficult to keep in tune. Harpists often spend as long as half an hour before a performance tuning their harps' strings so they produce exactly the right sounds.

Directions: Answer these questions about harps.

1. When were harps invented? _____

2. Where were harps invented? _____

3. What is a person called who plays the harp? _____

4. The harpist leans the harp against her

   ☐ right shoulder   ☐ left shoulder   ☐ left knee

5. How many pedals does a harp have?

   ☐ 5   ☐ 6   ☐ 7

6. Harps are easy to play.

   ☐ yes   ☐ no

Reading Comprehension

Recognizing Details: Brass Shows Class

If you like stirring music, you probably love the music made by brass instruments. Bright, loud, moving and magnificent — all these words describe the sounds made by brass.

Some of the earliest instruments were horns, and that's exactly what they were! Made from hollowed out animal horns, these primitive instruments could not possibly have made the rich sounds of modern horns which are made of brass.

Besides horns, modern brass bands have three other instruments: tubas, trombones and trumpets. Combined, these instruments can produce stirring marches as well as haunting melodies.

The most famous composer for brass instruments was John Phillip Sousa. Born in Washington, D.C. in 1854, Sousa, who died in 1932, was a military band conductor and composer. His music is still wildly popular. One of Sousa's most popular tunes for military bands was "Stars and Stripes Forever".

Besides composing band music, Sousa also invented a practical band instrument. The sousaphone is a huge tuba that makes very low notes. Because of the way it curls around the body, a sousaphone is easier to carry than a tuba. This is exactly why John Phillip Sousa invented it!

Directions: Answer these questions about brass instruments.

1. Who invented the sousaphone? _____

2. What were the first horns made from? _____

3. Where was John Phillip Sousa born? _____

4. When did John Phillip Sousa die? _____

5. Why did Sousa invent the sousaphone? _____
_____

6. How many types of instruments make up a modern brass band? _____

Reading Comprehension

Review

If you know anything about violin music, chances are you have heard the word "Stradivarius." (Strad-uh-vary-us.) Stradivarius is the name for the world's most magnificent violins. They are named after their creator, Antonio Stradivari.

Stradivari was born in northern Italy and lived from 1644 to 1737. Cremona, the town he lived in, was a place where violins were manufactured. Stradivari was very young when he learned to play the violin. He grew to love the instrument so much that he began to make them himself.

Violins were new instruments during Stradivari's time. People made them in different sizes and shapes and of different types of wood. Stradivari is said to have been very particular about the wood he selected for his violins. He took long walks alone in the forest to find just the right tree. He is also said to have used a secret and special type of varnish to put on the wood. Whatever the reasons, his violins are the best in the world.

Stradivari put such care and love into his violins that they are still used today. Many, of course, are in museums. But some wealthy musicians, who can afford the thousands and thousands of dollars they cost, own Stradivarius violins.

Stradivari passed his methods on to his sons. But the secrets of making Stradivarius violins seems to have died out with the family. Their rarity, as well as their mellow sound, make Stradivarius violins among the most prized instruments in the world.

Directions: Answer these questions about Stradivarius violins.

1. Where did Stradivari live?_____

2. What year did he die?_____

3. Why are Stradivarius violins special?

   _____

4. When was Stradivari born? _____

5. How did Stradivari select the wood for his violins?

   _____

6. Who else knew Stradivari's secrets for making such superior violins?

   _____

Reading Comprehension Name: _____

Sequencing: Little Bo-peep

Little Bo-peep has lost her sheep,
And can't tell where to find them.
"I'll leave them alone, and they'll come home,
Wagging their tails behind them."

Then Little Bo-peep dreamed of her sheep,
She dreamed she heard them bleating.
But when she awoke, she found it a joke,
For they were still a-fleeting.

Then up she took her little crook,
Determined for to find them.
She found them indeed,
but it made her heart bleed
For they'd left their tails behind them!

It happened one day that Bo-peep did stray
Into a meadow nearby,
She looked up in a tree, and what did she see?
Their tails all hung out to dry!

Bo-peep heaved a sigh and looked to the sky
As she gathered their tails up fast.
She ran to her sheep, they all gave a bleat
And said, "Our tails back at last!"

Directions: Number in order the events that occurred in the poem about Little Bo-peep.

_____ Little Bo-peep returns her sheep's tails to them.

_____ Little Bo-peep decides her sheep will find their ways home.

_____ Little Bo-peep lost her sheep.

_____ Little Bo-peep dreamed about her sheep.

_____ Little Bo-peep finds her sheep.

_____ Little Bo-peep finds her sheeps' tails in a tree.

Copyright © 1994 American Education Publishing Co.

Comprehension: All About Sheep

Did you ever wonder what really happened to the tails of Little Bo-peep's sheep? Here's the real story!

When sheep are born, they are called lambs. Lambs are born with long tails. A few days after lambs are born, the shepherd cuts off their tails. Because they get dirty, the lambs' long tails can pick up lots of germs. Cutting them off helps to prevent disease. The procedure is called "docking". This is probably exactly what happened to Bo-peep's sheep! Another shepherd must have cut their tails off without telling her.

Little lambs are cute. A lamb grows inside its mother for 150 days before it is born. This is called the "gestation period." Some types of sheep, such as hill sheep, give birth to one lamb at a time. Other types of sheep, such as lowland sheep, give birth to two or three lambs at a time.

After it is born, it takes a lamb three or four days to recognize its mother. Once it does, it stays close to her until it is about three weeks old. After that, the lamb becomes friendly toward other lambs.

Young lambs then form "play groups". They chase each other in circles. They butt into each other. Like children, they pretend to fight. When the play gets too rough, the lambs run back to their mothers for protection!

Lambs follow their mothers as they graze on grass. Usually, sheep move in single file behind an older female sheep. Female sheep are called ewes. The ewes teach their lambs how to keep themselves clean. This is called grooming. Sheep groom only their faces. Here is how they do it: they lick one of their front legs. Then they rub their faces against the spot they licked.

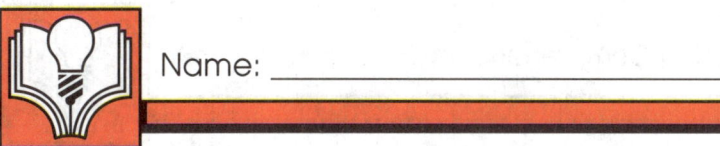

Directions: Answer these questions about sheep.

1. Define "docking".

_____

2. Name a type of sheep that gives birth to one lamb at a time. _____

3. Name a type of sheep that gives birth to two or three lambs at a time. _____

4. Female sheep are called

☐ grazers ☐ ewes ☐ dockers

5. Lambs begin playing in groups when they are

☐ 2 weeks old ☐ 3 weeks old ☐ 4 weeks old

Reading Comprehension   Name: _____

Following Directions: Little Boy Blue

Directions: Read "Little Boy Blue". Then work the puzzle.

Little Boy Blue, come blow your horn
The sheep's in the meadow, the cow's in the corn;
But where is the boy who looks after the sheep?
He's under a haystack, fast asleep!
Will you awake him? No, not I.
For if I do, he'll be sure to cry.

Across
3. This is where the sheep was.
5. What Little Boy Blue was asked to blow.
7. The other boy was fast _____.
8. Little Boy Blue was not asleep. He was ____.

Down
1. The boy who looks after the sheep slept here.
2. This is what the cow got into.
4. This is what the boy was supposed to be tending.
6. Did they wake the sleeping boy?

Reading Comprehension   Name: _____

Comprehension: Pigs Are Particular

Have you ever wondered why pigs wallow in the mud? It's not because they are dirty animals. Pigs have no sweat glands. They can't sweat, so they roll in the mud to cool themselves. The next time you hear anyone who's hot say, "I'm sweating like a pig!" be sure to correct him. Humans can sweat, but pigs cannot.

Actually, pigs are particular about their pens. They are very clean animals. They prefer to sleep in clean, dry places. They move their bowels and empty their bladders in another area. They do not want to get their homes dirty.

Another misconception about pigs is that they are smooth. Only cartoon pigs are pink, smooth and shiny-looking. The skin of real pigs is covered with bristles — small, stiff hairs. Their bristles protect their tender skin. When pigs are slaughtered, their bristles are sometimes made into hair or clothes brushes.

Female pigs are called sows. Sows have babies twice a year, and give birth to 10 to 14 piglets at a time. The babies have a "gestation period" of 16 weeks before they are born.

All the piglets together are called a "litter". Newborn piglets are on their tiny feet within a few minutes after birth. Can you guess why? They are hungrily looking for their mother's udders so they can get milk. As they nurse, piglets snuggle in close to their mother's udders to keep warm.

Directions: Answer these questions about pigs.

1. Why do pigs wallow in mud?

_____

2. How long is the gestation period for pigs? _____

3. What are pig bristles used for? _____

4. Tell two reasons pigs are on their feet soon after they are born.

1) _____

2) _____

5. A female pig is called a

☐ bristle   ☐ piglet   ☐ sow

6. Together, the newborn piglets are called a

☐ group   ☐ family   ☐ litter

Reading Comprehension

Name: _____

Context: No Kidding About Goats

Goats are independent creatures. Unlike sheep, which move easily in herds, goats cannot be driven along by a goatherd. They must be moved one or two at a time. Moving a big herd of goats can take a long time, so goatherds must be patient people.

Both male and female goats can have horns, but some goats are born without them. Male goats have beards but females do not. Male goats also have thicker and shaggier coats than females. During breeding season, when goats mate to produce babies, male goats have a very strong smell.

Goats are kept in paddocks with high fences. The fences are high because goats are high jumpers. They like to nibble on hedges and on the the tips of young trees. They can cause a lot of damage this way! That is why many farmers keep their goats in a paddock.

Baby goats are called "kids" and two or three at a time are born to the mother goat. Farmers usually begin to bottle-feed kids when they are a few days old. They milk the mother goat and keep the milk. Goat's milk is much easier to digest than cow's milk, and many people think it tastes delicious.

Directions: Answer these questions about goats.

1. Use context clues to choose the correct definition of "goatherd".
   ☐ person who herds goats
   ☐ goats in a herd
   ☐ person who has heard of goats

2. Use context clues to choose the correct definition of "paddock".

   ☐ pad   ☐ fence   ☐ pen

3. Use context clues to choose the correct definition of "nibble".
   ☐ take small bites
   ☐ take small drinks
   ☐ take little sniffs

4. Use context clues to choose the correct definition of "delicious".

   ☐ delicate   ☐ tasty   ☐ terrible

Reading Comprehension  Name: _____

Comprehension: Cows Are Complicated Creatures

If you believe cows have four stomachs, you're right! It sounds incredible, but it's true.

Here are the "hows" and "whys" of a cow's digestive system: First, it's important to know that cows do not have upper front teeth. They eat grass by wrapping their tongues around it and pulling it from the ground. They do have back teeth, but still they cannot properly chew the grass.

Cows swallow grass without chewing it up. When it's swallowed, the grass goes into the cow's first stomach, called a "rumen" (roo-mun). There, it is broken up by the digestive juices and forms into a ball of grass. This ball is called a "cud". The cow is able to bring the cud back up into its mouth. Then, the cow chews the cud into a pulp with its back teeth and re-swallows it.

After it is swallowed the second time, the cud goes into the cow's second stomach. This second stomach is called the "reticulum" (re-tick-u-lum). The reticulum filters the food to take out any small stones or other non-food matter. Then it passes the food onto the cow's third stomach. The third stomach is called the "omasum" (oh-mass-um).

From there, any food that is still undigested is sent back to the first stomach so the cow can bring it back up into her mouth and chew it some more. The rest goes into the cow's fourth stomach. The fourth stomach is called the "abomasum" (ab-oh-ma-sum). Digesting food that can be turned into milk is a full-time job for cows!

Directions: Answer these questions about cows.

1. List in order the names of a cow's four stomachs.

1) _____ 2) _____

3) _____ 4) _____

2. What is the name of the ball of grass a cow chews on? _____

3. A cow has no

☐ bottom teeth   ☐ top teeth   ☐ fourth stomach

4. This stomach acts as a filter for digestion.

☐ reticulum   ☐ rumen   ☐ abomasum

Reading Comprehension Name: _____

Context: Dairy Cows

Some cows are raised for their beef. Other cows, called dairy cows, are raised for their milk. A dairy cow cannot produce any milk until after its first calf is born. Cows are not mature enough to give birth until they are two years old.

A cow's gestation period is 40 weeks long and she usually gives birth to one calf. Then she produces a lot of milk to feed it. When the calf is two days old, the dairy farmer takes the calf away from its mother. After that, the cow is milked twice a day.

The dairy cow's milk comes from the large, smooth udder beneath its body. The udder has four openings called teats. To milk the cow, the farmer grasps a teat and squeezes it with his thumb and forefinger. Then he gently but firmly pulls his hand down the teat to squeeze the milk out. Milking machines that are hooked to the cow's teats to duplicate this action can milk many cows quickly.

A dairy cow's milk production is not at the same level all the time. When the cow is pregnant, milk production gradually decreases. For two months before her calf is born, a cow is said to be "dry" and is not milked. This happens because, like humans, much of the cow's food is actually being used to nourish the unborn calf.

Farmers give the cow extra food at this time to make sure the mother and unborn calf are well-nourished. Again, like humans, well-nourished mother cows are more likely to produce healthy babies.

Directions: Answer these questions about cows' milk production.

1. Use context clues to choose the correct definition of "grasp".

   ☐ pull firmly   ☐ hold firmly   ☐ hold gently

2. Use context clues to choose the correct definition of "duplicate".

   ☐ correct   ☐ make   ☐ copy

3. Use context clues to choose the correct definition of "decreases".

   ☐ becomes more   ☐ becomes less   ☐ becomes quicker

4. Use context clues to choose the correct definition of "nourish".

   ☐ to be happy   ☐ to be friendly   ☐ to feed

ANSWER KEY

This Answer Key has been designed so that it may be easily removed if you so desire.

GRADE 5 READING COMPREHENSION

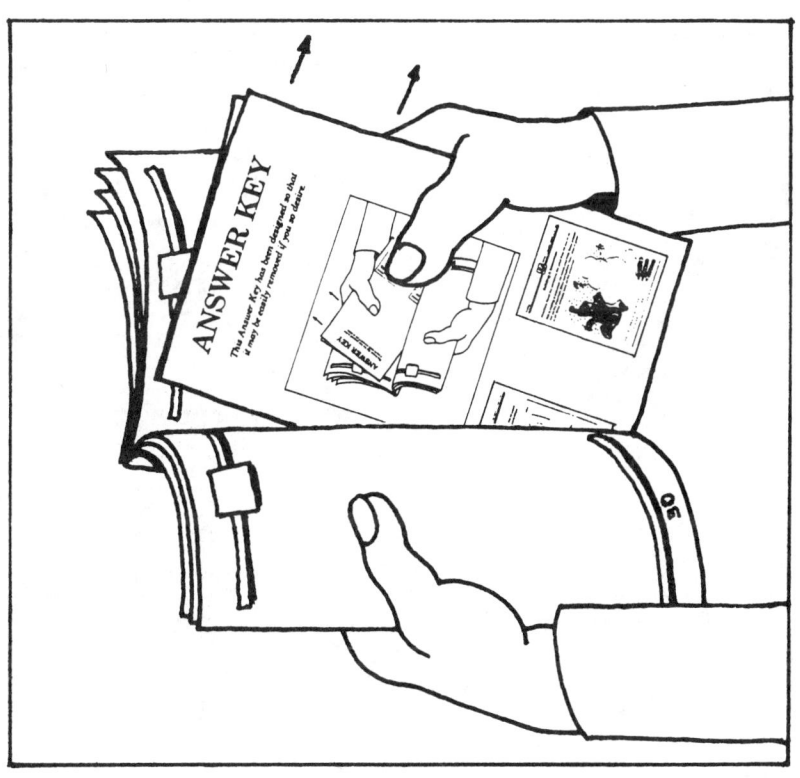

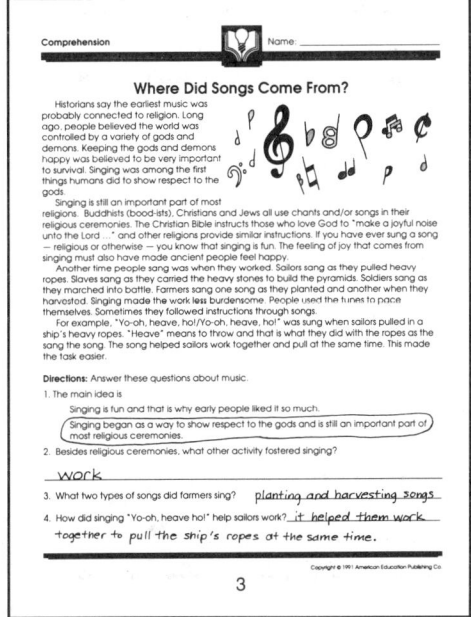

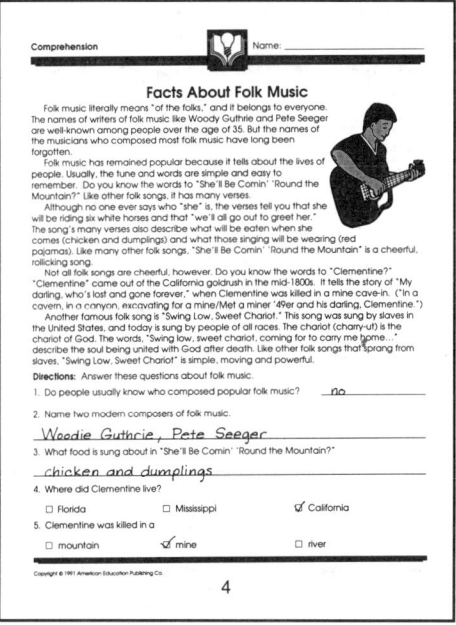

Jazz Notes

Jazz, which began in the southern United States, became popular in the late 1800s. Like some folk songs, jazz was the music made by black people. It was the music of former slaves.

The rhythm and the beat of early jazz reflected the roots of black Americans in Africa. Many early jazz musicians could not read music. They sometimes made up their music as they went along on their clarinets, trumpets and other instruments. This "on the spot composing" is called "improvising." Modern jazz musicians carry on this tradition of improvising.

To improvise, a musician's grasp of music must go far beyond technical understanding. A jazz musician really must put a little of his own heart into what he plays. If you have ever seen jazz musicians at work, you know that the effort and joy they put into their music is enormous. Two of the most famous jazz musicians are trumpet players Louis Armstrong and Miles Davis.

Jazz music is often upbeat. It reflects the musicians' joy in living. Have you ever heard the expression, "Let's jazz this up?" To "jazz up" means to make something livelier. Even if you have never heard jazz played, you can imagine it must be anything but dreary!

Four to ten musicians usually make up a jazz band. Besides the trumpet and clarinet, a jazz band may include drums, piano, bass guitar, and sometimes a saxophone, violin and flute.

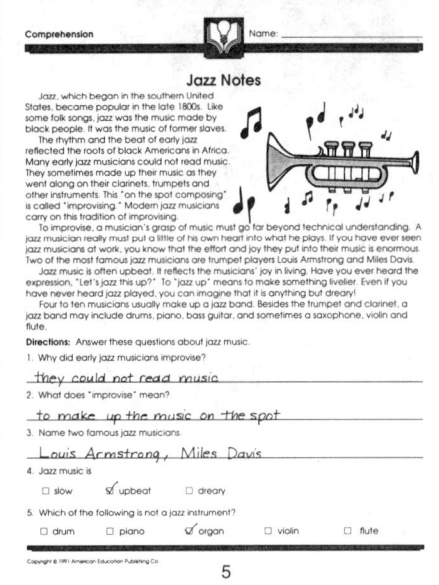

Directions: Answer these questions about jazz music.

1. Why did early jazz musicians improvise?
   they could not read music
2. What does "improvise" mean?
   to make up the music on the spot
3. Name two famous jazz musicians.
   Louis Armstrong, Miles Davis
4. Jazz music is
   ☐ slow ☑ upbeat ☐ dreary
5. Which of the following is not a jazz instrument?
   ☐ drum ☐ piano ☑ organ ☐ violin ☐ flute

Brass Shows Class

If you like stirring music, you probably love the music made by brass instruments. Bright, loud, moving and magnificent — all these words describe the sounds made by brass.

Some of the earliest instruments were horns, and that's exactly what they were! Made from hollowed out animal horns, these primitive instruments could not possibly have made the rich sounds of modern horns which are made of brass.

Besides horns, modern brass bands have three other instruments: tubas, trombones and trumpets. Combined, these instruments can produce stirring marches as well as haunting melodies.

The most famous composer for brass instruments was John Phillip Sousa. Born in Washington, D.C. in 1854, Sousa, who died in 1932, was a military band conductor and composer. His music is still widely popular. One of Sousa's most popular tunes for military bands was "Stars and Stripes Forever."

Besides composing band music, Sousa also invented a practical band instrument. The sousaphone is a huge tuba that makes very low notes. Because of the way it curls around the body, a sousaphone is easier to carry than a tuba. This is exactly why John Phillip Sousa invented it!

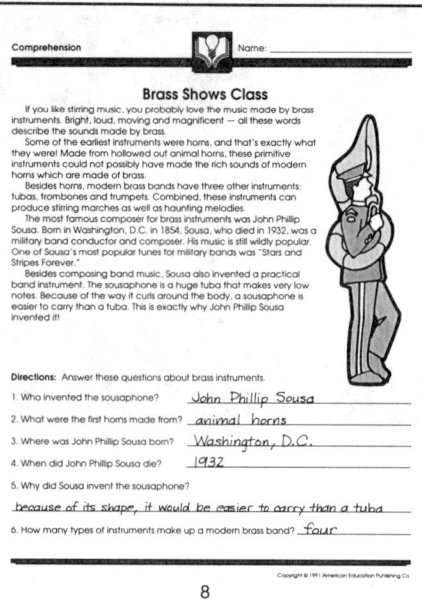

Directions: Answer these questions about brass instruments.

1. Who invented the sousaphone? _John Phillip Sousa_
2. What were the first horns made from? _animal horns_
3. Where was John Phillip Sousa born? _Washington, D.C._
4. When did John Phillip Sousa die? _1932_
5. Why did Sousa invent the sousaphone?
   because of its shape, it would be easier to carry than a tuba
6. How many types of instruments make up a modern brass band? _four_

Flutes, Oboes, Clarinets, Bassoons

There are four kinds of woodwind instruments in modern bands. They are flutes, oboes, clarinets and bassoons. They are called "woodwind" instruments for two sensible reasons. In the beginning, they were all made of wood. Also, the musician's breath, or "wind" was required to play them.

Although they are all woodwinds, these instruments look different and are played differently. To play an oboe, the musician blows through a mouthpiece on the front of the instrument. The mouthpiece, called a "reed," is made of two flat pieces of a kind of wood called cane. Clarinet players also blow into a reed mouthpiece. The clarinet has only one reed in its mouthpiece.

To play the flute, the musician blows across the hole. The way the breath is aimed helps to make the flute's different sounds. The bassoon is the largest woodwind instrument. Bassoon players blow through a short metal pipe before it goes into the body of the bassoon. It makes a very different sound than the clarinet or the oboe.

Woodwind instruments also have keys — but not the kind that open locks. These keys are more like levers that the musician pushes up and down. The levers cover holes. When the musician pushes down on the lever, it closes that hole. When she lifts her finger, it opens the hole. Different sounds are produced by controlling the amount of breath, or "wind," that goes through the holes.

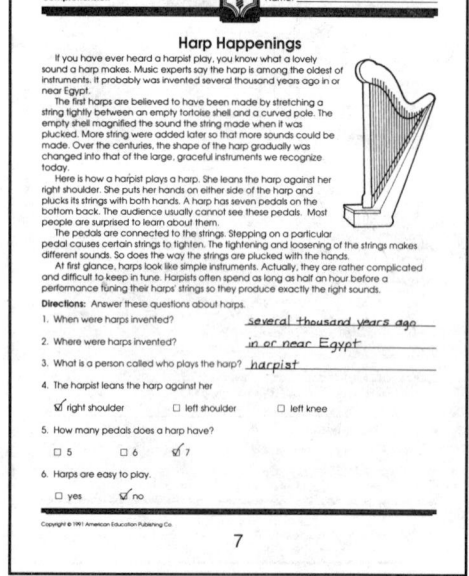

Directions: Answer these questions about woodwind instruments.

1. What instruments are in the woodwind section?
   flute, bassoon, oboe, clarinet
2. Why are some instruments called woodwinds?
   in the beginning, they were all made of wood, and "wind" (breath) is needed to play them
3. How is a flute different from the other woodwinds?
   the musician blows across the holes instead of into a mouthpiece
4. When a musician pushes down on a woodwind key, what happens?
   it closes the hole beneath the key
5. How would a woodwind musician open the holes on her instrument?
   lift her fingers

Review

If you know anything about violin music, chances are you have heard the word "Stradivarius." (Strad-uh-vary-us.) Stradivarius is the name for the world's most magnificent violins. They are named after their creator, Antonio Stradivari.

Stradivari was born in northern Italy and lived from 1644 to 1737. Cremona, the town he lived in, was a place where violins were manufactured. Stradivari was very young when he learned to play the violin. He grew to love the instrument so much that he began to make them himself.

Violins were new instruments during Stradivari's time. People made them in different sizes and shapes and of different types of wood. Stradivari is said to have been very particular about the wood he selected for his violins. He took long walks wildly in the forest to find just the right type of tree. He is also said to have used a secret and special type of varnish to put on the wood. Whatever the reasons, his violins are the best in the world.

Stradivari put such care and love into his violins, that they are still used today. Many, of course, are in museums. But some wealthy musicians who can afford the thousands and thousands of dollars being asked for them, own Stradivarius violins.

Stradivari passed his methods on to his sons. But the secrets of making Stradivarius violins seems to have died out with the family. Their rarity, as well as their mellow sound, make Stradivarius violins among the most prized instruments in the world.

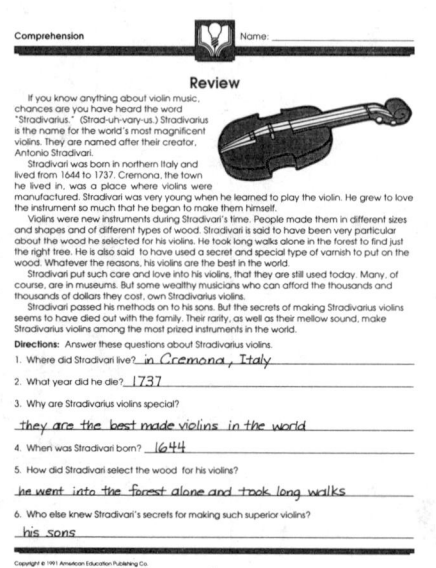

Directions: Answer these questions about Stradivarius violins.

1. Where did Stradivari live? _in Cremona, Italy_
2. What year did he die? _1737_
3. Why are Stradivarius violins special?
   they are the best made violins in the world
4. When was Stradivari born? _1644_
5. How did Stradivari select the wood for his violins?
   he went into the forest alone and took long walks
6. Who else knew Stradivari's secrets for making such superior violins?
   his sons

Harp Happenings

If you have ever heard a harpist play, you know what a lovely sound a harp makes. Music experts say the harp is among the oldest of instruments. It probably was invented several thousand years ago in or near Egypt.

The first harps are believed to have been made by stretching string tightly between an empty tortoise shell and a curved pole. The empty shell magnified the sound the string made when it was plucked. More strings were added later so that more sounds could be made. Over the centuries, the shape of the harp gradually was changed into that of the large, graceful instruments we recognize today.

Here is how a harpist plays a harp. First, she leans the harp against her right shoulder. She puts her hands on either side of the harp and plucks its strings with both hands. A harp has seven pedals on the bottom back. The audience usually cannot see these pedals. Most people are surprised to learn about them.

The pedals are connected to the strings. Stepping on a particular pedal causes certain strings to tighten. The tightening and loosening of the strings makes different sounds. So does the way the strings are plucked with the hands.

At first glance, harps look like simple instruments. Actually, they are rather complicated and difficult to keep in tune. Harpists often spend as long as half an hour before a performance fixing their harp's strings so they produce exactly the right sounds.

Directions: Answer these questions about harps.

1. When were harps invented? _several thousand years ago_
2. Where were harps invented? _in or near Egypt_
3. What is a person called who plays the harp? _harpist_
4. The harpist leans the harp against her
   ☑ right shoulder ☐ left shoulder ☐ left knee
5. How many pedals does a harp have?
   ☐ 5 ☐ 6 ☑ 7
6. Harps are easy to play.
   ☐ yes ☑ no

Little Bo-peep

Little Bo-peep has lost her sheep,
And can't tell where to find them.
"I'll leave them alone, and they'll come home,
Wagging their tails behind them."

Then Little Bo-peep dreamed of her sheep,
She dreamed she heard them bleating.
But when she awoke, she found it a joke,
For they were still a-fleeting.

Then up she took her little crook,
Determined for to find them.
She found them indeed,
but it made her heart bleed
For they'd left their tails behind them!

It happened one day that Bo-peep did stray
Into a meadow nearby,
She looked up in a tree, and what did she see?
Their tails all hung out to dry!

Bo-peep heaved a sigh and looked to the sky
As she gathered their tails up fast.
She ran to her sheep, they all gave a bleat
And said, "Our tails back at last!"

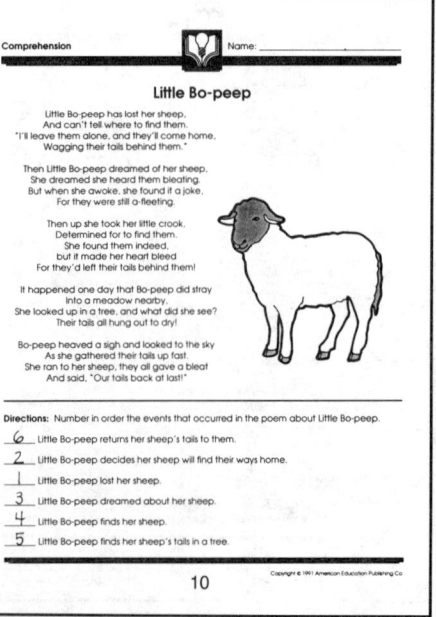

Directions: Number in order the events that occurred in the poem about Little Bo-peep.

_6_ Little Bo-peep returns her sheep's tails to them.
_2_ Little Bo-peep decides her sheep will find their ways home.
_1_ Little Bo-peep lost her sheep.
_3_ Little Bo-peep dreamed about her sheep.
_4_ Little Bo-peep finds her sheep.
_5_ Little Bo-peep finds her sheep's tails in a tree.

All About Sheep

Did you ever wonder what really happened to the tails of Little Bo-peep's sheep? Here's the real story!

When sheep are born, they are called lambs. Lambs are born with long tails. A few days after lambs are born, the shepherd cuts off their tails. Because they get dirty, the lambs' long tails can pick up lots of germs. Cutting them off helps to prevent disease. The procedure is called "docking." This is probably exactly what happened to Bo-peep's sheep! Another shepherd must have cut their tails off without telling her.

Little lambs are cute. A lamb grows inside its mother for 150 days before it is born. This is called the "gestation period." Some types of sheep, such as hill sheep, give birth to one lamb at a time. Other types of sheep, such as lowland sheep, give birth to two or three lambs at a time.

After it is born, it takes a lamb three or four days to recognize its mother. Once it does, it stays close to her until it is about three weeks old. After that, the lamb becomes friendly toward other lambs.

Young lambs then form "play groups." They chase each other in circles. They butt into each other. Like children, they pretend to fight. When the play gets too rough, the lambs run back to their mothers for protection!

Lambs follow their mothers as they graze on grass. Usually, sheep move in single file behind an older female sheep. Female sheep are called ewes. The ewes teach their lambs how to keep themselves clean. This is called grooming. Sheep groom only their faces. Here is how they do it: they lick one of their front legs. Then they rub their faces against the spot they licked.

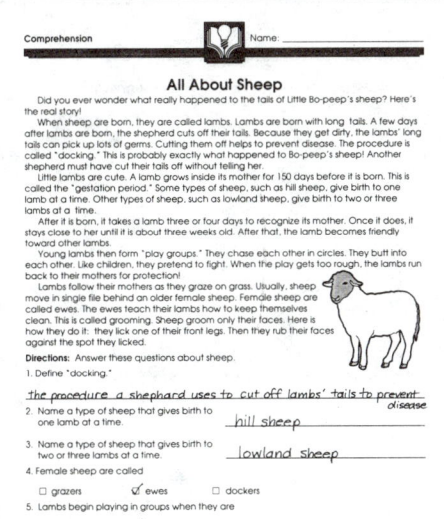

Directions: Answer these questions about sheep.

1. Define "docking."
   the procedure a shephard uses to cut off lambs' tails to prevent disease
2. Name a type of sheep that gives birth to one lamb at a time. _hill sheep_
3. Name a type of sheep that gives birth to two or three lambs at a time. _lowland sheep_
4. Female sheep are called
   ☐ grazers   ☑ ewes   ☐ dockers
5. Lambs begin playing in groups when they are
   ☐ 2 weeks old   ☑ 3 weeks old   ☐ 4 weeks old

11

No Kidding About Goats

Goats are independent creatures. Unlike sheep, which move easily in herds, goats cannot be driven along by a goatherd. They must be moved one or two at a time. Moving a big herd of goats can take a long time, so goatherds must be patient people.

Both male and female goats can have horns, but some goats are born without them. Male goats have beards but females do not. Male goats also have thicker and shaggier coats than females. During breeding season, when goats mate to produce babies, male goats have a very strong smell.

Goats are kept in paddocks with high fences. The fences are high because goats are high jumpers. They like to nibble on hedges and on the tips of young trees. They can cause a lot of damage this way! That is why many farmers keep their goats in a paddock.

Baby goats are called "kids" and two or three at a time are born to the mother goat. Farmers usually begin to bottle-feed kids when they are a few days old. They milk the mother goat and keep the milk. Goat's milk is much easier to digest than cow's milk, and many people think it tastes delicious.

Directions: Answer these questions about goats.

1. Use context clues to choose the correct definition of "goatherd."
   ☑ person who herds goats
   ☐ goats in a herd
   ☐ person who's heard of goats
2. Use context clues to choose the correct definition of "paddock."
   ☐ pad   ☐ fence   ☑ pen
3. Use context clues to choose the correct definition of "nibble."
   ☑ take small bites
   ☐ take small drinks
   ☐ take little sniffs
4. Use context clues to choose the correct definition of "delicious."
   ☐ delicate   ☑ tasty   ☐ terrible

14

Little Boy Blue

Directions: Read "Little Boy Blue." Then work the puzzle.

Little Boy Blue, come blow your horn
The sheep's in the meadow, the cow's in the corn;
But where is the boy who looks after the sheep?
He's under a haystack, fast asleep!
Will you awake him? No, not I.
For if I do, he'll be sure to cry.

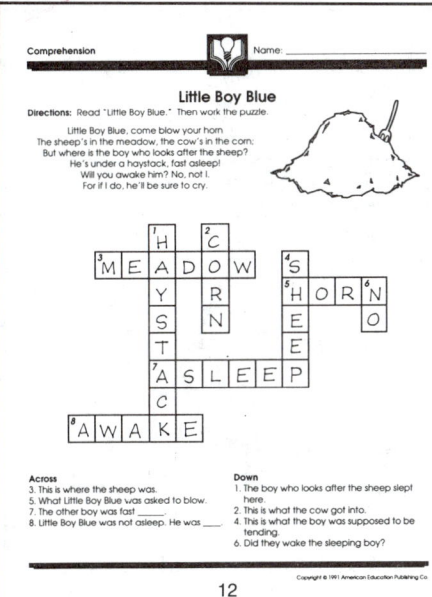

[Crossword puzzle with answers:
3. MEADOW
5. HORN
7. ASLEEP
8. AWAKE
Down: HAYSTACK, CORN, SHEEP]

Across
3. This is where the sheep was.
5. What Little Boy Blue was asked to blow.
7. The other boy was fast ___.
8. Little Boy Blue was not asleep. He was ___.

Down
1. The boy who looks after the sheep slept here.
2. This is what the cow got into.
4. This is what the boy was supposed to be tending.
6. Did they wake the sleeping boy?

12

Cows Are Complicated Creatures

If you believe cows have four stomachs, you're right! It sounds incredible, but it's true.

Here are the "hows" and "whys" of a cow's digestive system: First, it's important to know that cows do not have upper front teeth. They eat grass by wrapping their tongues around it and pulling it from the ground. They do have back teeth, but still they cannot properly chew the grass.

Cows swallow grass without chewing it up. When it's swallowed, the grass goes into the cow's first stomach, called a "rumen" (roo-mun). There, it is broken up by the digestive juices and forms into a ball of grass. This ball is called a "cud." The cow is able to bring the cud back up into its mouth. Then, the cow chews the cud into a pulp with its back teeth and re-swallows it.

After it is swallowed the second time, the cud goes into the cow's second stomach. This second stomach is called the "reticulum" (re-tick-u-lum). The reticulum filters the food to take out any small stones or other non-food matter. Then it passes the food onto the cow's third stomach. The third stomach is called the "omasum" (oh-mas-um).

From there, any food that is still undigested is sent back to the first stomach so the cow can bring it back up in her mouth and chew it some more. The rest goes into the cow's fourth stomach. The fourth stomach is called the "abomasum" (ab-oh-ma-sum). Digesting food that can be turned into milk is a full-time job for cows!

Directions: Answer these questions about cows.

1. List in order the names of a cow's four stomachs.
   1) _rumen_   2) _reticulum_
   3) _omasum_   4) _abomasum_
2. What is the name of the ball of grass a cow chews on? _cud_
3. A cow has no
   ☐ bottom teeth   ☑ top teeth   ☐ fourth stomach
4. This stomach acts as a filter for digestion.
   ☑ reticulum   ☐ rumen   ☐ abomasum

15

Pigs Are Particular

Have you ever wondered why pigs wallow in the mud? It's not because they are dirty animals. Pigs have no sweat glands. They can't sweat, so they roll in the mud to cool themselves. The next time you hear anyone who's hot say, "I'm sweating like a pig!" be sure to correct him. Humans can sweat, but pigs cannot.

Actually, pigs are particular about their pens. They are very clean animals. They prefer to sleep in clean, dry places. They move their bowels and empty their bladders in another area. They do not want to get their homes dirty.

Another misconception about pigs is that they are smooth. Only cartoon pigs are pink, smooth and shiny-looking. The skin of real pigs is covered with bristles — small, stiff hairs. Their bristles protect their tender skin. When pigs are slaughtered, their bristles are sometimes made into hair or clothes brushes.

Female pigs are called sows. Sows have babies twice a year, and give birth to 10 to 14 piglets at a time. The babies have a "gestation period" of 16 weeks before they are born. All the piglets together are called a "litter." Newborn piglets are on their feet within a few minutes after birth. Can you guess why? They are hungrily looking for their mother's udders so they can get milk. As they nurse, piglets snuggle in close to their mother's udders to keep warm.

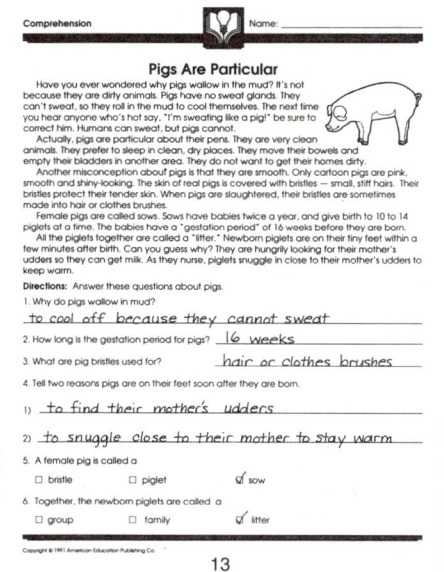

Directions: Answer these questions about pigs.

1. Why do pigs wallow in mud?
   to cool off because they cannot sweat
2. How long is the gestation period for pigs? _16 weeks_
3. What are pig bristles used for? _hair or clothes brushes_
4. Tell two reasons pigs are on their feet soon after they are born.
   1) _to find their mother's udders_
   2) _to snuggle close to their mother to stay warm_
5. A female pig is called a
   ☐ bristle   ☐ piglet   ☑ sow
6. Together, the newborn piglets are called a
   ☐ group   ☐ family   ☑ litter

13

Dairy Cows

Some cows are raised for their beef. Other cows, called dairy cows, are raised for their milk. A dairy cow cannot produce any milk until after its first calf is born. Cows are not mature enough to give birth until they are two years old.

A cow's gestation period is 40 weeks long and she usually gives birth to one calf. Then she produces a lot of milk to feed it. When the calf is two days old, the dairy farmer takes the calf away from its mother. After that, the cow is milked twice a day.

The dairy cow's milk comes from the large, smooth udder beneath its body. The udder has four openings called teats. To milk the cow, the farmer grasps a teat and squeezes it with his thumb and forefinger. Then he gently but firmly pulls his hand down then the teat to pull the milk out. Milking machines that are hooked to the cow's teats to duplicate this action can milk many cows quickly.

A dairy cow's milk production is not at the same level all the time. When the cow is pregnant, milk production gradually decreases. For two months before her calf is born, the cow is said to be "dry" and is not milked. This happens because, like humans, much of the cow's food is actually being used to nourish the unborn calf.

Farmers give the cow extra food at this time to make sure the mother and unborn calf are well-nourished. Again, like humans, well-nourished mother cows are more likely to produce healthy babies.

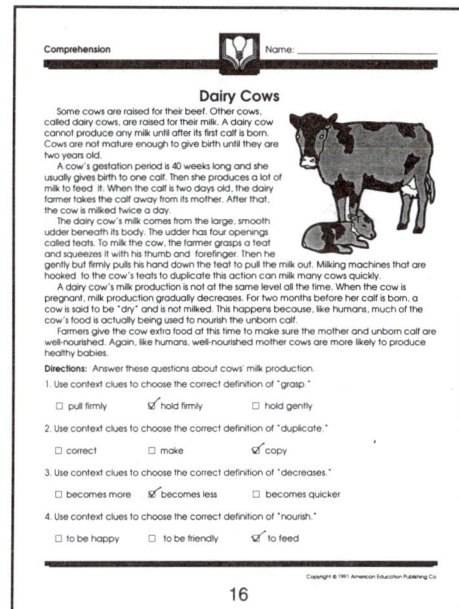

Directions: Answer these questions about cows' milk production.

1. Use context clues to choose the correct definition of "grasp."
   ☐ pull firmly   ☑ hold firmly   ☐ hold gently
2. Use context clues to choose the correct definition of "duplicate."
   ☐ correct   ☐ make   ☑ copy
3. Use context clues to choose the correct definition of "decreases."
   ☐ becomes more   ☑ becomes less   ☐ becomes quicker
4. Use context clues to choose the correct definition of "nourish."
   ☐ to be happy   ☐ to be friendly   ☑ to feed

16

Review

Have you ever heard the expression "pecking order?" In the pecking order of a school, the principal is at the top of the order. Next comes the assistant principal, then the teachers and students.

In the pecking order of chickens, the most aggressive chicken is the leader. The leader is the hen that uses her beak most often to peck the chickens she bosses. These chickens, in turn, boss other chickens by pecking them, and so on. Chickens can peck all others who are "below" them in the pecking order. They never peck those "above" themselves by pecking their bosses. And you thought chickens were dumb!

Directions: Answer these questions about chickens.

1. Put this pecking order of 4 chickens in proper sequence.
   _2_ This chicken pecks numbers 3 and 4 but never number 1.
   _1_ No one pecks this chicken. She's the top boss.
   _4_ This chicken can't peck anyone.
   _3_ This chicken pecks chicken number 4.

2. Use the context of the first two sentences in the second paragraph to figure out what "aggressive" means.
   bossy / mean

3. Look at your answer to number 1. Give directions to chicken number 3 on who she can peck and why.
   peck only chicken number 4 because everyone else is above you in the pecking order

4. Who is at the top of the pecking order in a school?
   principal

Where Some Words Got Their Meanings

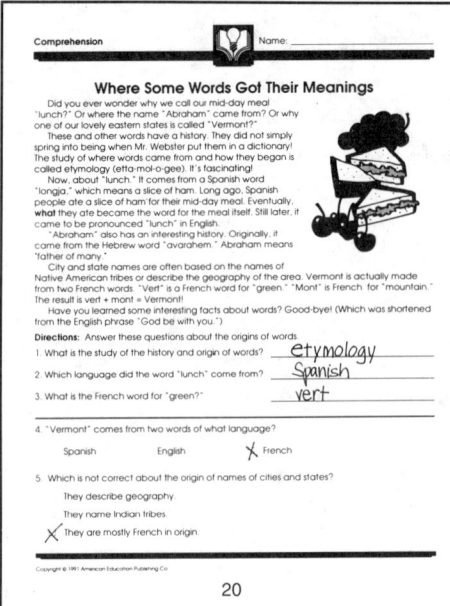

Did you ever wonder why we call our mid-day meal "lunch." Or where the name "Abraham" came from? Or why one of our lovely eastern states is called "Vermont?"

These and other words have a history. They did not simply spring into being when Mr. Webster put them in a dictionary! The study of where words came from and how they began is called etymology (etta-mol-o-gee). It's fascinating!

Now, about "lunch." It comes from a Spanish word "longia," which means a slice of ham. Long ago, Spanish people ate a slice of ham for their mid-day meal. Eventually, what they ate became the word for the meal itself. Still later, it came to be pronounced "lunch" in English.

"Abraham" also has an interesting history. Originally, it came from the Hebrew word "avarahem." Abraham means "father of many."

City and state names are often based on the names of Native American tribes or describe the geography of the area. Vermont is actually made from two French words. "Vert" is a French word for "green." "Mont" is French for "mountain." The result is vert + mont = Vermont!!

Have you learned some interesting facts about words? Good-bye! (Which was shortened from the English phrase "God be with you.")

Directions: Answer these questions about the origins of words.

1. What is the study of the history and origin of words? etymology
2. Which language did the word "lunch" come from? Spanish
3. What is the French word for "green?" vert

4. "Vermont" comes from two words of what language?
   ☐ Spanish   ☐ English   ✗ French

5. Which is not correct about the origin of names of cities and states?
   ☐ They describe geography
   ☐ They name Indian tribes.
   ✗ They are mostly French in origin.

Books, Books And More Books!

Variety is said to be the spice of life. Where books are concerned, variety is the key to reading pleasure. There is a type of book to appeal to every reader.

Science fiction, gothic stories and historical novels are among the types of fiction books favored by many children. (Gothic stories are about people who lived during the Middle Ages, between 600 and 1500 A.D.) Many children who like nonfiction choose books about animals, careers, sports and hobbies.

Each year, hundreds of new books are published for children on these and other topics. A popular series of books for girls between the ages of 8 and 12 is *Sweet Valley Kids* written by Francine Pascal. Another new book by Pascal is *Sweet Valley Twins Chiller*. All Pascal's books are fiction stories about children who live in the town of Sweet Valley.

If you like legends, an interesting book is *Dream Wolf* by Paul Goble. *Dream Wolf* is a retelling of an old Indian legend. Legends may or may not be true. They are stories passed down from one generation to another. Some legends are scary! *The Legend of Sleepy Hollow*, for example, is about a "headless horseman." Other legends are about a person's brave or amazing deeds. For example, there are many legends about Robin Hood, who stole from the rich and gave to the poor. Because they are handed down through the generations, most legends began long ago.

Many people like to read nonfiction books, which are about things that really exist or really happened. Those interested in information about Native Americans might to read these books: *The Navajos* by Peter Iverson, *The Yakima* by Helen Schuster, and *The Creek* by Michael Green. The titles of these nonfiction books are names of Indian tribes.

Directions: Answer these questions about the many types of books.

1. What time period is covered by gothic books?
   the Middle Ages, between 600 to 1500 A.D.

2. What is the name of Francine Pascal's series of books?
   Sweet Valley Kids

3. What legend is about a headless horseman?
   The Legend of Sleepy Hollow

Which of the following is **not** correct about legends.
   ☐ Legends are passed down through the generations.
   ✓ Most legends are true.
   ☐ Most legends began long ago.

Fact Or Opinion?

A fact can be proved. An opinion tells what someone thinks, feels or believes. An opinion can't be proved.

(1) What to do about homeless people has become an important issue in most big cities. (2) Some people believe federal money should be spent to provide housing. (3) Others think the people should somehow find a way to take care of themselves. (4) Among those raising money for the homeless are bookstores. (5) In Los Angeles, for example, a group called "Booksellers and Writers Against Homelessness" held a series of fundraisers for homeless people. (6) What a wonderful thing for these people to do! (7) The *Los Angeles Daily News* also helped bring public attention to the homeless through a front-page article. (8) The article told about a shelter for homeless women in the San Fernando Valley that was in desperate need of funds. (9) As a result of the article, hundreds of people sent donations to the shelter. (10) Americans are very generous!

Directions: Read the numbered sentences above and, in the corresponding numbered blanks, tell whether each sentence gives a fact or an opinion.

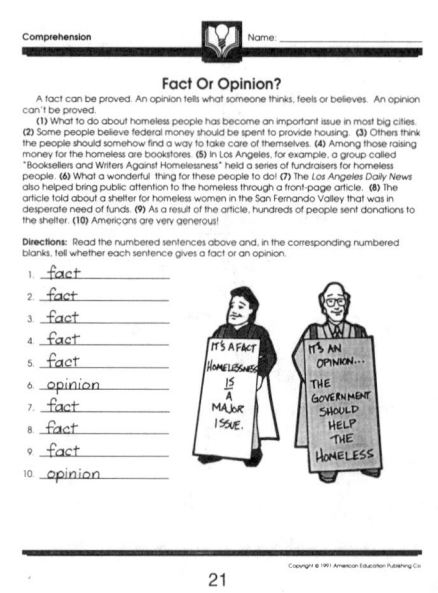

1. fact
2. fact
3. fact
4. fact
5. fact
6. opinion
7. fact
8. fact
9. fact
10. opinion

Context

Directions: Read the sentences. Use the context clues to figure out the meanings of the bold words. Then put checkmarks beside the correct meanings.

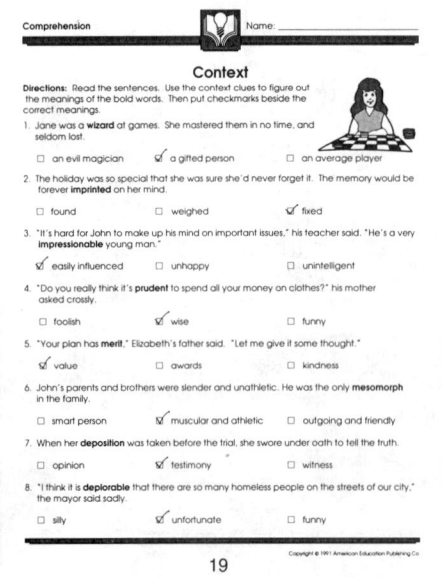

1. Jane was a **wizard** at games. She mastered them in no time, and seldom lost.
   ☐ an evil magician   ✓ a gifted person   ☐ an average player

2. The holiday was so special that she was sure she'd never forget it. The memory would be forever **imprinted** on her mind.
   ☐ found   ☐ weighed   ✓ fixed

3. "It's hard for John to make up his mind on important issues," his teacher said. "He's a very **impressionable** young man."
   ✓ easily influenced   ☐ unhappy   ☐ unintelligent

4. "Do you really think it's **prudent** to spend all your money on clothes?" his mother asked crossly.
   ☐ foolish   ✓ wise   ☐ funny

5. "Your plan has **merit**," Elizabeth's father said. "Let me give it some thought."
   ✓ value   ☐ awards   ☐ kindness

6. John's parents and brothers were slender and unathletic. He was the only **mesomorph** in the family.
   ☐ smart person   ✓ muscular and athletic   ☐ outgoing and friendly

7. When her **deposition** was taken before the trial, she swore under oath to tell the truth.
   ☐ opinion   ✓ testimony   ☐ witness

8. "I think it is **deplorable** that there are so many homeless people on the streets of our city," the mayor said sadly.
   ☐ silly   ✓ unfortunate   ☐ funny

Help For The Homeless

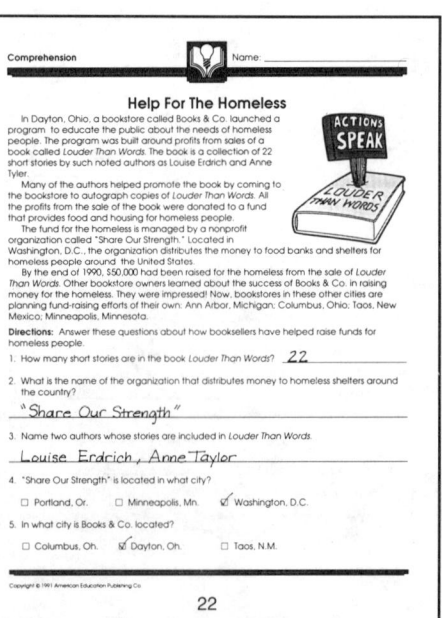

In Dayton, Ohio, a bookstore called Books & Co. launched a program to educate the public about the needs of homeless people. The program was built around profits from sales of a book called *Louder Than Words*. The book is a collection of 22 short stories by such noted authors as Louise Erdrich and Anne Tyler.

Many of the authors helped promote the book by coming to the bookstore to autograph copies of *Louder Than Words*. All the profits from the sale of the book were donated to a fund that provides food and housing for homeless people.

The fund for the homeless is managed by a nonprofit organization called "Share Our Strength." Located in Washington, D.C., the organization distributes the money to food banks and shelters for homeless people around the United States.

By the end of 1990, $50,000 had been raised for the homeless from the sale of *Louder Than Words*. Other bookstore owners learned about the success of Books & Co. in raising money for the homeless. They were impressed! Now, bookstores in these other cities are planning fund-raising efforts of their own: Ann Arbor, Michigan; Columbus, Ohio; Taos, New Mexico; Minneapolis, Minnesota.

Directions: Answer these questions about how booksellers have helped raise funds for homeless people.

1. How many short stories are in the book *Louder Than Words*? 22

2. What is the name of the organization that distributes money to homeless shelters around the country?
   "Share Our Strength"

3. Name two authors whose stories are included in *Louder Than Words*.
   Louise Erdrich, Anne Taylor

4. "Share Our Strength" is located in what city?
   ☐ Portland, Or.   ☐ Minneapolis, Mn.   ✓ Washington, D.C.

5. In what city is Books & Co. located?
   ☐ Columbus, Oh.   ✓ Dayton, Oh.   ☐ Taos, N.M.

Books On "Reading Rainbow"

Have you ever seen "Reading Rainbow" on your local public television station? (1) It's a show about books and its host is LeVar Burton. (2) LeVar is very handsome and the show is great!

Some books that have been featured on the show are *I Can Be an Oceanographer* by Paul Sipiera, *Soccer Sam* by Jean Marzollo, *Redbird* by Patrick Fort and *Miss Nelson Has a Field Day* by Harry Allard. (3) *Miss Nelson Has a Field Day* sounds like the most interesting book of all!

(4) On "Reading Rainbow," children give informal book reports about books they have read. (5) All the children are adorable! In about one minute, each child describes his or her book. (6) While the child is talking, pictures of some of the pages from the book are shown. (7) Seeing the pictures will make you want to read the book. A few books are described on each show. (8) Other activities include trips with LeVar to places the books tell about. (9) Every child should make time to watch "Reading Rainbow!" (10) It's a fabulous show!

Directions: Read the numbered sentences above and, in the corresponding numbered blanks, tell whether each sentence gives a fact or an opinion.

1. fact
2. opinion
3. opinion
4. fact
5. opinion
6. fact
7. opinion
8. fact
9. opinion
10. opinion

23

Books For Kids Are Big Business

Between 1978 and 1988, the number of children's books published in the United States doubled. The publishing (1) **industry**, which prints, promotes and sells books, does not usually move this fast. Why? Because if publishers print too many books that don't sell, they lose money. They like to wait, if they can, to see what the "public demand" is for certain types of books. Then they accept manuscripts from writers who have written the types of books the public seems to want. (2) More than 4,600 children's books were published in 1988 because publishers thought they could sell that many titles. Many copies of each title were printed and sold to bookstores and libraries. (3) The publishers made good profits and, since then, the number of children's books published each year has continued to grow.

The title of a recent new book for children is *The Wild Horses of Sweetbriar* by Natalie Kinsey-Warnock. (4) It is the story of a girl and a band of wild horses that lived on an island off the coast of Massachusetts in 1903. (5) The story sounds very exciting! (6) Mustangs can be quite dangerous. (7) The plot of *The Wild Horses of Sweetbriar* is probably filled with danger and suspense.

Directions: Answer these questions about the numbered words and sentences in the corresponding numbered blanks about how interest in writing, reading and selling children's books has grown.

1. Use context clues to choose the correct definition of "industry."
   ☐ book sellers ☐ writers ☑ entire business

2. If 4,600 books were sold in 1988, how many books were sold in 1978? **2,300**

3. Fact or opinion: The number of children's books published each year has continued to grow. **fact**

4. Fact or opinion: *The Wild Horses of Sweetbriar* is the story of a girl and the wild horses that lived on an island in 1903. **fact**

5. Fact or opinion: The story sounds very exciting! **opinion**

6. Use context clues to choose the correct definition of "mustangs."
   ☐ pet horses ☑ wild horses ☐ island horses

7. Fact or opinion: The plot of *The Wild Horses of Sweetbriar* is probably filled with danger and suspense. **opinion**

24

Chunky Tomato And Green Onion Sauce

Ingredients
- 2 tablespoons corn oil
- 2 cloves garlic, finely chopped
- 1 1/2 pound plum tomatoes, cored, peeled, seeded, then coarsely chopped
- 3 green onions, cut in half lengthwise, then thinly sliced
- salt and freshly ground pepper

Heat oil in a heavy skillet over medium heat. Add garlic and cook until yellow, about one minute. Stir in tomatoes. Season with salt and pepper. Cook until thickened, about 10 minutes. Stir in green onions and serve.

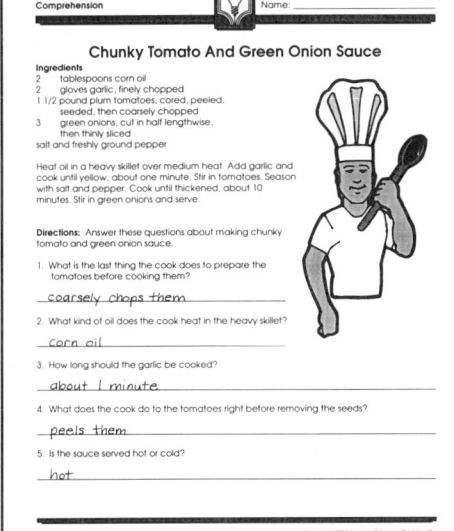

Directions: Answer these questions about making chunky tomato and green onion sauce.

1. What is the last thing the cook does to prepare the tomatoes before cooking them?
   coarsely chops them

2. What kind of oil does the cook heat in the heavy skillet?
   corn oil

3. How long should the garlic be cooked?
   about 1 minute

4. What does the cook do to the tomatoes right before removing the seeds?
   peels them

5. Is the sauce served hot or cold?
   hot

25

Cooking With Care

People are so busy these days that many people have no time to cook. This creates a problem, because most families love home cooking! The food tastes good and warm, and a family meal brings everyone together. In some families, meals are often the only times everyone sees one another at the same time.

Another reason people enjoy home cooking is that it is often a way of showing love. A parent who bakes a batch of chocolate chip cookies isn't just satisfying a child's sweet tooth. She (or he!) is sending a message. The message says, "I care about you enough to spend an hour making cookies that you will eat up in 15 minutes if I let you!"

There's also something about the odor of good cooking that appeals to people of all ages. It makes most of us feel secure and loved — even if **we** are the ones doing the cooking! Next time you smell a cake baking, stop for a moment and pay attention to your mood. Chances are, the good smell is making you feel happy.

Real estate agents know that good cooking smells are important. They sometimes advise people whose homes are for sale to bake cookies or bread if prospective buyers are coming to see the house. The good smells make the place "feel like home." These pleasant smells help to convince prospective buyers that the house would make a good home for **their** family, too!

Directions: Answer these questions about good cooking.

1. Why do fewer people cook nowadays?
   many people are too busy

2. Why are family meals important?
   they are sometimes the only time the family is together

3. What do homemade cookies do besides satisfy a child's sweet tooth?
   show someone cares enough to spend the time to bake them

4. Real estate agents often advise home sellers holding open houses to
   ☐ bake muffins and pies ☑ bake cookies or bread

5. The smell of baking at open houses encourages buyers to
   ☐ bake cookies ☑ buy the house ☐ bake bread

26

Chocolate Chunk Cookies

These chocolate chunk cookies require only five ingredients. Before you combine them, preheat the oven to 350 degrees. Preheating the oven to the correct temperature is always step number 1 in baking.

Now, into a large mixing bowl, empty an 18 and 1/4 oz. package of chocolate fudge cake mix (any brand). Add a 10-ounce package of semi-sweet chocolate broken into small pieces, two 5 and 1/8-ounce packages of chocolate fudge pudding mix (any brand), and 1/2 cup chopped walnuts. Use a large wooden spoon to combine the ingredients. When they are well-mixed, add 1 and 1/2 cups of mayonnaise and stir thoroughly. Shape the dough into small balls and place the balls two inches apart on an ungreased cookie sheet. Bake 12 minutes. Cool and eat!

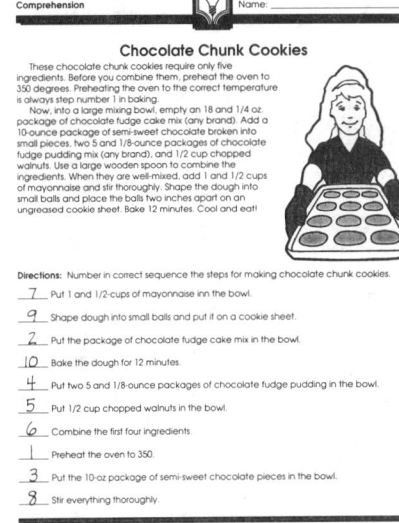

Directions: Number in correct sequence the steps for making chocolate chunk cookies.

- **7** Put 1 and 1/2 cups of mayonnaise in the bowl.
- **9** Shape dough into small balls and put it on a cookie sheet.
- **2** Put the package of chocolate fudge cake mix in the bowl.
- **10** Bake the dough for 12 minutes.
- **4** Put two 5 and 1/8-ounce packages of chocolate fudge pudding in the bowl.
- **5** Put 1/2 cup chopped walnuts in the bowl.
- **6** Combine the first four ingredients.
- **1** Preheat the oven to 350.
- **3** Put the 10-oz package of semi-sweet chocolate pieces in the bowl.
- **8** Stir everything thoroughly.

27

Eating High-Fiber Cereal Helps Dieters

Have you heard your parents or other adults talk about "high fiber" diets? Foods that are high in fiber, like oats and other grains, are believed to be very healthful.

Here's why: The fiber adds bulk to the food the body digests and helps keep the large intestine working properly. Corn, apples, celery, nuts and other chewy foods also contain fiber to help keep the body's systems for digesting and eliminating food working properly.

Researchers at the University of Minnesota have found another good reason to eat high fiber food, especially at breakfast. Because fiber is bulky, it absorbs a lot of liquid in the stomach. As it absorbs the liquid, it swells. This "fools" the stomach into thinking it's full. As a result, when lunchtime comes, those who have eaten a high fiber breakfast are not as hungry. They eat less food at lunch. Without much effort on their parts, dieters eating a high fiber breakfast can lose weight.

The university researchers say a person could lose 10 pounds in a year, just by eating a high fiber breakfast! This is good news to people who are only slightly overweight and want an easy method for losing that extra 10 pounds.

Directions: Answer these questions about eating cereal.

1. Why is fiber healthful? **It adds bulk to the food the body digests and helps keep the large intestine working properly.**

2. How does fiber "fool" the stomach? **It swells when it absorbs liquids in the stomach and fools the stomach into thinking it's full.**

3. How does "fooling" the stomach help people lose weight? **Their stomach doesn't feel as empty and they eat less food.**

4. How many pounds could a dieter eating a high-fiber breakfast lose in a year?
   ☐ 20 pounds ☐ 30 pounds ☑ 10 pounds

5. The university that did the research is in which state?
   ☐ Michigan ☑ Minnesota ☐ Montana

28

New Corn

I will clothe myself in spring clothing
And visit the slopes of the eastern hill.
By the mountain stream, a mist hovers,
Hovers a moment and then scatters.
Then comes a wind blowing from the south
That brushes the fields of new corn.

Directions: Answer these questions about the ancient poem called "New Corn" translated from the Chinese language.

1. The main idea is:
   - (The poet will dress comfortably and go to where the corn grows so he can enjoy the beauty of nature.) ✓
   - The poet will dress comfortably and visit the slopes of the eastern hill, where he will plant corn.

2. Which way is the wind blowing?
   south

3. Where does the mist hover?
   by the mountain stream

4. What do you think the poet means by "spring clothing?"
   clothes that are not heavy like winter clothes

Chinese Cabbage

Many Americans enjoy Chinese food. In big cities, like New York and Chicago, many Chinese restaurants deliver their food in small boxes to homes. It's just like ordering a pizza! Then the people who ordered the "take-out" food simply open it, put it on their plates and eat it while it's hot.

Because it tastes so good, many people are curious about the ingredients in Chinese food. **Siu choy** and **choy sum** are two types Chinese cabbage that many people enjoy eating. **Siu choy** grows to be two- or three-feet around! Of course, it is chopped into small pieces before it is cooked and served. Its leaves are light green and soft. It is not crunchy like American cabbage. **Siu choy** is used in soups and stews. Sometimes it is pickled with vinegar and other ingredients and served as a side dish to other courses.

Choy sum is looks and tastes different from **siu choy**. **Choy sum** grows to be only 8 to 10 inches long. It is a flowering cabbage that grows small yellow flowers. The flowers are "edible," which means they can be eaten. Its leaves are long and bright green. After its leaves are boiled for four minutes, **Choy sum** is often served as a salad. Oil and oyster sauce are mixed together and poured over **choy sum** as a salad dressing.

Directions: Answer the questions about Chinese cabbage.

1. Which Chinese cabbage grows small yellow flowers? choy sum
2. Which Chinese cabbage is served as a salad? choy sum
3. Is **siu choy** crunchy? no
4. What ingredients are in the salad dressing used on **choy sum**? oil and oyster sauce
5. What size does **siu choy** grow to be? two- to three-feet around
6. Name two main dishes **siu choy** is used in. soups and stews

---

The French Eat Differently

Many people believe that French people are very different from Americans. This is certainly true where eating habits are concerned! According to a report by the World Health Organization, each year the French people eat four times more butter than Americans. The French also eat twice as much cheese! In addition, they eat more vegetables, potatoes, grain and fish.

Yet, despite the fact that they eat **larger** amounts of these foods, the French take in about the same number of calories each day as Americans. (French and American men consume about 2,500 calories each day. French and American women take in about 1,600 calories daily.)

How can this be? If the French are eating more of certain types of foods, shouldn't this add up to more calories? And why are so few French people overweight compared to Americans? The answer: Americans consume **18 times** more refined sugar than the French, and drink twice as much whole milk!

Although many Americans believe the French wind up each meal with grand and gooey desserts, this just isn't so. Except for special occasions, dessert in a typical French home consists of fresh fruit or cheese. Many American families, on the other hand, like to end their meals with a bowl or two of ice cream or another sweet treat.

It's believed that this difference in the **kind** of calories consumed — rather than in the total **number** of calories taken in — is what causes many Americans to be chubby and most French people to be skinny.

Directions: Answer these questions about the eating habits of French and American people.

1. Name six types of foods the French people eat more of each year than Americans.
   butter, cheese, potatoes, fish, vegetables, grains
2. How many calories does the average French man eat each day? 2,500
3. How much whole milk does the average French person drink compared to the average American? half as much
4. How much more refined sugar do Americans eat than the French?
   ☐ 2 times more ☑ 18 times more ☐ 15 times more
5. What do French families usually eat for dessert?
   ☐ French gooey ☐ ice cream ☑ fruit and cheese

Review

Here's a recipe for a special mashed potatoes treat that serves two people. The recipe is fast and easy to follow and the results are delicious!

Begin by peeling two large potatoes and cooking them in a pot of boiling water. When a fork or knife inserted into them pulls out easily, you will know they are done. Then take them from the pot and drain them well. Put them in a large mixing bowl and add 2 tablespoons of milk and 2 tablespoons of butter. Mash with a potato masher until the lumps are gone.

Then in a skillet, melt a tablespoon of butter and add 1 bunch of chopped green onions. Cook them about one minute. Add them to the potatoes and mix gently. Season with salt and pepper and add more butter if desired. Serve and eat!

Directions: Answer these questions about how to make mashed potatoes with green onions.

1. The main idea is:
   - (This recipe, which has only 4 ingredients (plus salt and pepper) is fast and easy and the potatoes are delicious.) ✓
   - This recipe, which has only 5 ingredients (plus salt and pepper) is fast and easy, and the potatoes are delicious.

2. Name the main ingredients in this recipe (not including salt and pepper).
   potatoes, milk, butter, green onions

3. How many people does this recipe serve? two

4. Number the following sequence of steps correctly.
   4 Cook the chopped green onion for 1 minute.
   1 Peel two potatoes.
   6 Season with salt and pepper and serve.
   3 Put the cooked potatoes in a bowl with milk and butter, then mash.
   5 Add the onion to the mashed potatoes.
   2 Boil the potatoes until they are done.

5. Give directions on what to do with the cooked potatoes after they are put in the bowl and before the green onions are added. Add 2 tablespoons of milk, 2 tablespoons of butter and mash until the lumps are gone.

Reading Comprehension

Name: _____

Review

Have you ever heard the expression "pecking order"? In the pecking order of a school, the principal is at the top of the order. Next comes the assistant principal, then the teachers and students.

In the pecking order of chickens, the most aggressive chicken is the leader. The leader is the hen that uses her beak most often to peck the chickens she bosses. These chickens, in turn, boss other chickens by pecking them, and so on. Chickens can peck all others who are "below" them in the pecking order. They never peck "above" themselves by pecking their bosses. And you thought chickens were dumb!

Directions: Answer these questions about chickens.

1. Put this pecking order of 4 chickens in proper sequence.

   _____ This chicken pecks numbers 3 and 4 but never number 1.

   _____ No one pecks this chicken. She's the top boss.

   _____ This chicken can't peck anyone.

   _____ This chicken pecks chicken number 4.

2. Use the context of the first two sentences in the second paragraph to figure out what "aggressive" means.

   _____

3. Look at your answer to number 1. Give directions to chicken number 3 on who she can peck and why.

   _____

4. Who is at the top of the pecking order in a school?

   _____

Reading Comprehension

Name: _____

Comprehension: Books, Books And More Books!

Variety is said to be the spice of life. Where books are concerned, variety is the key to reading pleasure. There is a type of book to appeal to every reader.

Science fiction, gothic stories and historical novels are among the types of fiction books favored by many children. (Gothic stories are about people who lived during the Middle Ages, between 600 and 1500 A.D.) Many children who like nonfiction choose books about animals, careers, sports and hobbies.

Each year, hundreds of new books are published for children on these and other topics. A popular series of books for girls between the ages of 8 and 12 is *Sweet Valley Kids* written by Francine Pascal. Another new book by Pascal is *Sweet Valley Twins Chiller*. All Pascal's books are fictional stories about children who live in the town of Sweet Valley.

If you like legends, an interesting book is *Dream Wolf* by Paul Goble. *Dream Wolf* is a retelling of an old Native American legend. Legends may or may not be true. They are stories passed down from one generation to another. Some legends are scary! The *Legend of Sleepy Hollow*, for example, is about a "headless horseman". Other legends are about a person's brave or amazing deeds. For example, there are many legends about Robin Hood, who stole from the rich and gave to the poor. Because they are handed down through the generations, most legends began long ago.

Many people like to read nonfiction books, which are about things that really exist or really happened. Those interested in information about Native Americans might like to read these books: *The Navajos* by Peter Iverson, *The Yakima* by Helen Schuster, and *The Creek* by Michael Green. The titles of these nonfiction books are names of Native American tribes.

Directions: Answer these questions about the many types of books.

1. What time period is covered by gothic books?

   _____

2. What is the name of Francine Pascal's series of books?

   _____

3. What legend is about a headless horseman?

   _____

Which of the following is **not** correct about legends.
- ☐ Legends are passed down through the generations.
- ☐ Most legends are true.
- ☐ Most legends began long ago.

Reading Comprehension

Context

Directions: Read the sentences. Use the context clues to figure out the meanings of the bold words. Then put checkmarks beside the correct meanings.

1. Jane was a **wizard** at games. She mastered them in no time, and seldom lost.

   ☐ an evil magician ☐ a gifted person ☐ an average player

2. The holiday was so special that she was sure she'd never forget it. The memory would be forever **imprinted** on her mind.

   ☐ found ☐ weighed ☐ fixed

3. "It's hard for John to make up his mind on important issues," his teacher said. "He's a very **impressionable** young man."

   ☐ easily influenced ☐ unhappy ☐ unintelligent

4. "Do you really think it's **prudent** to spend all your money on clothes?" his mother asked crossly.

   ☐ foolish ☐ wise ☐ funny

5. "Your plan has **merit**," Elizabeth's father said. "Let me give it some thought."

   ☐ value ☐ awards ☐ kindness

6. John's parents and brothers were slender and unathletic. He was the only **mesomorph** in the family.

   ☐ smart person ☐ muscular and athletic ☐ outgoing and friendly

7. When her **deposition** was taken before the trial, she swore under oath to tell the truth.

   ☐ opinion ☐ testimony ☐ witness

8. "I think it is **deplorable** that there are so many homeless people on the streets of our city," the mayor said sadly.

   ☐ silly ☐ unfortunate ☐ funny

Reading Comprehension   Name: _____

Comprehension: Where Words Get Their Meanings

Did you ever wonder why we call our mid-day meal "lunch"? Or where the name "Abraham" came from? Or why one of our lovely eastern states is called "Vermont"?

These and other words have a history. They did not simply spring into being when Mr. Webster put them in a dictionary! The study of where words came from and how they began is called etymology (etta-mol-o-gee). It's fascinating!

Now, about "lunch". It comes from a Spanish word "longja", which means a slice of ham. Long ago, Spanish people ate a slice of ham for their mid-day meal. Eventually, **what** they ate became the word for the meal itself. Still later, it came to be pronounced "lunch" in English.

"Abraham" also has an interesting history. Originally, it came from the Hebrew word "avarahem". Abraham means "father of many".

City and state names are often based on the names of Native American tribes or describe the geography of the area. Vermont is actually made from two French words. "Vert" is a French word for "green". "Mont" is French for "mountain".

Have you learned some interesting facts about words? Good-bye! (Which was shortened from the English phrase "God be with you".)

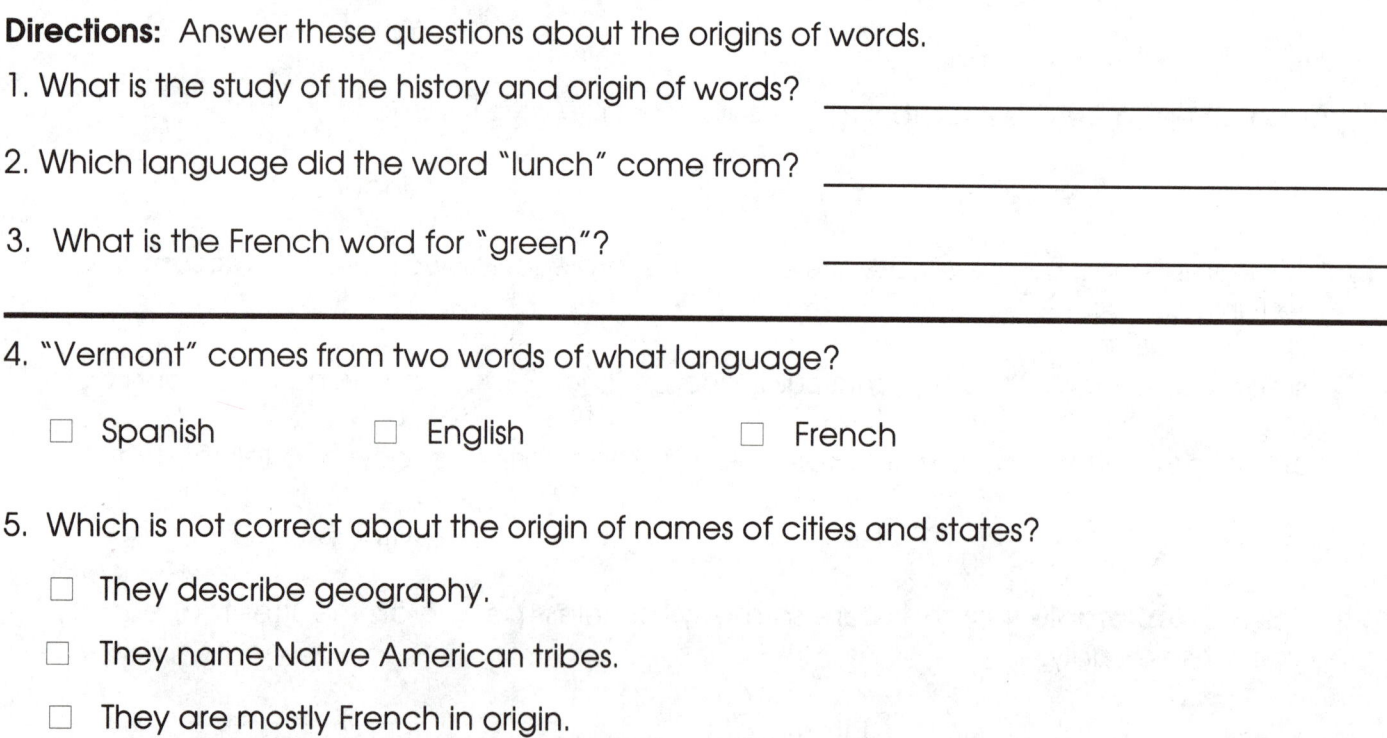

Directions: Answer these questions about the origins of words.

1. What is the study of the history and origin of words? _____

2. Which language did the word "lunch" come from? _____

3. What is the French word for "green"? _____

4. "Vermont" comes from two words of what language?

   ☐ Spanish   ☐ English   ☐ French

5. Which is not correct about the origin of names of cities and states?

   ☐ They describe geography.

   ☐ They name Native American tribes.

   ☐ They are mostly French in origin.

Reading Comprehension   Name: _____

Fact Or Opinion?

A fact can be proved. An opinion tells what someone thinks, feels or believes. An opinion can't be proved.

(1) What to do about homeless people has become an important issue in most big cities. **(2)** Some people believe federal money should be spent to provide housing. **(3)** Others think the people should somehow find a way to take care of themselves. **(4)** Among those raising money for the homeless are bookstores. **(5)** In Los Angeles, for example, a group called "Booksellers and Writers Against Homelessness" held a series of fundraisers for homeless people. **(6)** What a wonderful thing for these people to do! **(7)** The *Los Angeles Daily News* also helped bring public attention to the homeless through a front-page article. **(8)** The article told about a shelter for homeless women in the San Fernando Valley that was in desperate need of funds. **(9)** As a result of the article, hundreds of people sent donations to the shelter. **(10)** Americans are very generous!

Directions: Read the numbered sentences above and, in the corresponding numbered blanks, tell whether each sentence gives a fact or an opinion.

1. _____
2. _____
3. _____
4. _____
5. _____
6. _____
7. _____
8. _____
9. _____
10. _____

Reading Comprehension   Name: _____

Comprehension: Help For The Homeless

In Dayton, Ohio, a bookstore called Books & Co. launched a program to educate the public about the needs of homeless people. The program was built around profits from sales of a book called *Louder Than Words*. The book is a collection of 22 short stories by such noted authors as Louise Erdrich and Anne Tyler.

Many of the authors helped promote the book by coming to the bookstore to autograph copies of *Louder Than Words*. All the profits from the sale of the book were donated to a fund that provides food and housing for homeless people.

The fund for the homeless is managed by a nonprofit organization called "Share Our Strength". Located in Washington, D.C., the organization distributes the money to food banks and shelters for homeless people around the United States.

By the end of 1990, $50,000 had been raised for the homeless from the sale of *Louder Than Words*. Other bookstore owners learned about the success of Books & Co. in raising money for the homeless. They were impressed! Now, bookstores in these other cities are planning fund-raising efforts of their own: Ann Arbor, Michigan; Columbus, Ohio; Taos, New Mexico; Minneapolis, Minnesota.

Directions: Answer these questions about how booksellers have helped raise funds for homeless people.

1. How many short stories are in the book *Louder Than Words*? _____

2. What is the name of the organization that distributes money to homeless shelters around the country?

_____

3. Name two authors whose stories are included in *Louder Than Words*.

_____

4. "Share Our Strength" is located in what city?

   ☐ Portland, Or.   ☐ Minneapolis, Mn.   ☐ Washington, D.C.

5. In what city is Books & Co. located?

   ☐ Columbus, Oh.   ☐ Dayton, Oh.   ☐ Taos, N.M.

Fact Or Opinion: "Reading Rainbow"

Have you ever seen "Reading Rainbow" on your local public television station? **(1)** It's a show about books and its host is LeVar Burton. **(2)** LeVar is very handsome and the show is great!

Some books that have been featured on the show are *I Can Be an Oceanographer* by Paul Sipiera, *Soccer Sam* by Jean Marzolla, *Redbird* by Patrick Fort and *Miss Nelson Has a Field Day* by Harry Allard. **(3)** *Miss Nelson Has a Field Day* sounds like the most interesting book of all!

(4) On "Reading Rainbow," children give informal book reports about books they have read. **(5)** All the children are adorable! In about one minute, each child describes his or her book. **(6)** While the child is talking, pictures of some of the pages from the book are shown. **(7)** Seeing the pictures will make you want to read the book. A few books are described on each show. **(8)** Other activities include trips with LeVar to places the books tell about. **(9)** Every child should make time to watch "Reading Rainbow"! **(10)** It's a fabulous show!

Directions: Read the numbered sentences above and, in the corresponding numbered blanks, tell whether each sentence gives a fact or an opinion.

1. _____
2. _____
3. _____
4. _____
5. _____
6. _____
7. _____
8. _____
9. _____
10. _____

Reading Comprehension Name: _____

Review: Books For Kids Are Big Business

Between 1978 and 1988, the number of children's books published in the United States doubled. The publishing **(1) industry**, which prints, promotes and sells books, does not usually move this fast. Why? Because if publishers print too many books that don't sell, they lose money. They like to wait, if they can, to see what the "public demand" is for certain types of books. Then they accept manuscripts from writers who have written the types of books the public seems to want. **(2)** More than 4,600 children's books were published in 1988 because publishers thought they could sell that many titles. Many copies of each title were printed and sold to bookstores and libraries. **(3)** The publishers made good profits and, since then, the number of children's books published each year has continued to grow.

The title of a recent new book for children is *The Wild Horses of Sweetbriar* by Natalie Kinsey-Warnock. **(4)** It is the story of a girl and a band of wild horses that lived on an island off the coast of Massachusetts in 1903. **(5)** The story sounds very exciting! **(6)** Mustangs can be quite dangerous. **(7)** The plot of *The Wild Horses of Sweetbriar* is probably filled with danger and suspense.

Directions: Answer these questions about the numbered words and sentences in the corresponding numbered blanks about how interest in writing, reading and selling children's books has grown.

1. Use context clues to choose the correct definition of "industry".

   ☐ book sellers   ☐ writers   ☐ entire business

2. If 4,600 books were sold in 1988, how many books were sold in 1978? _____

3. Fact or opinion: The number of children's books published each
   year has continued to grow.   _____

4. Fact or opinion: *The Wild Horses of Sweetbriar* is the story of a girl
   and the wild horses that lived on an island in 1903.   _____

5. Fact or opinion: The story sounds very exciting!   _____

6. Use context clues to choose the correct definition of "mustangs".

   ☐ pet horses   ☐ wild horses   ☐ island horses

7. Fact or opinion: The plot of *The Wild Horses of Sweetbriar* is
   probably filled with danger and suspense.   _____

Following Directions: Chunky Tomato And Green Onion Sauce

Ingredients
- 2 tablespoons corn oil
- 2 cloves garlic, finely chopped
- 1 1/2 pound plum tomatoes, cored, peeled, seeded, then coarsely chopped
- 3 green onions, cut in half lengthwise, then thinly sliced
- salt and freshly ground pepper

Heat oil in a heavy skillet over medium heat. Add garlic and cook until yellow, about one minute. Stir in tomatoes. Season with salt and pepper. Cook until thickened, about 10 minutes. Stir in green onions and serve.

Directions: Answer these questions about making chunky tomato and green onion sauce.

1. What is the last thing the cook does to prepare the tomatoes before cooking them?

   _____

2. What kind of oil does the cook heat in the heavy skillet?

   _____

3. How long should the garlic be cooked?

   _____

4. What does the cook do to the tomatoes right before removing the seeds?

   _____

5. Is the sauce served hot or cold?

   _____

Reading Comprehension

Name: _____

Comprehension: Cooking With Care

People are so busy these days that many people have no time to cook. This creates a problem, because most families love home cooking! The food tastes good and warm, and a family meal brings everyone together. In some families, meals are often the only times everyone sees one another at the same time.

Another reason people enjoy home cooking is that it is often a way of showing love. A parent who bakes a batch of chocolate chip cookies isn't just satisfying a child's sweet tooth. She or he is sending a message. The message says, "I care about you enough to spend an hour making cookies that you will eat up in 15 minutes if I let you!"

There's also something about the odor of good cooking that appeals to people of all ages. It makes most of us feel secure and loved — even if **we** are the ones doing the cooking! Next time you smell a cake baking, stop for a moment and pay attention to your mood. Chances are, the good smell is making you feel happy.

Real estate agents know that good cooking smells are important. They sometimes advise people whose homes are for sale to bake cookies or bread if prospective buyers are coming to see the house. The good smells make the place "feel like home". These pleasant smells help to convince potential buyers that the house would make a good home for **their** family, too!

Directions: Answer these questions about good cooking.

1. Why do fewer people cook nowadays?

_____

2. Why are family meals important?

_____

3. What do homemade cookies do besides satisfy a child's sweet tooth?

_____

4. Real estate agents often advise home sellers holding open houses to

　☐ clean the garage　　　　☐ bake cookies or bread

5. The smell of baking at open houses encourages buyers to

　☐ bake cookies　　　☐ buy the house　　　☐ bake bread

Reading Comprehension   Name: _____

Sequencing: Chocolate Chunk Cookies

These chocolate chunk cookies require only five ingredients. Before you combine them, preheat the oven to 350 degrees. Preheating the oven to the correct temperature is always step number 1 in baking.

Now, into a large mixing bowl, empty an 18 and 1/4 oz. package of chocolate fudge cake mix (any brand). Add a 10-ounce package of semi-sweet chocolate broken into small pieces, two 5 and 1/8-ounce packages of chocolate fudge pudding mix (any brand), and 1/2 cup chopped walnuts. Use a large wooden spoon to combine the ingredients. When they are well-mixed, add 1 and 1/2 cups of mayonnaise and stir thoroughly. Shape the dough into small balls and place the balls two inches apart on an ungreased cookie sheet. Bake 12 minutes. Cool and eat!

Directions: Number in correct sequence the steps for making chocolate chunk cookies.

_____ Put 1 and 1/2-cups of mayonnaise in the bowl.

_____ Shape dough into small balls and put it on a cookie sheet.

_____ Put the package of chocolate fudge cake mix in the bowl.

_____ Bake the dough for 12 minutes.

_____ Put two 5 and 1/8-ounce packages of chocolate fudge pudding in the bowl.

_____ Put 1/2 cup chopped walnuts in the bowl.

_____ Combine the first four ingredients.

_____ Preheat the oven to 350.

_____ Put the 10-oz package of semi-sweet chocolate pieces in the bowl.

_____ Stir everything thoroughly.

Reading Comprehension   Name: _____

Comprehension: Eating High-Fiber Cereal Helps Dieters

Have you heard your parents or other adults talk about "high fiber" diets? Foods that are high in fiber, like oats and other grains, are believed to be very healthful.

Here's why: The fiber adds bulk to the food the body digests and helps keep the large intestine working properly. Corn, apples, celery, nuts and other chewy foods also contain fiber to help keep the body's systems for digesting and eliminating food working properly.

Researchers at the University of Minnesota have found another good reason to eat high fiber food, especially at breakfast. Because fiber is bulky, it absorbs a lot of liquid in the stomach. As it absorbs the liquid, it swells. This "fools" the stomach into thinking it's full. As a result, when lunchtime comes, those who have eaten a high fiber breakfast are not as hungry. They eat less food at lunch. Without much effort on their parts, dieters eating a high fiber breakfast can lose weight.

The university researchers say a person could lose 10 pounds in a year, just by eating a high fiber breakfast! This is good news to people who are only slightly overweight and want an easy method for losing that extra 10 pounds.

Directions: Answer these questions about eating cereal.

1. Why is fiber healthful?

_____

2. How does fiber "fool" the stomach?

_____

3. How does "fooling" the stomach help people lose weight?

_____

4. How many pounds could a dieter eating a high-fiber breakfast lose in a year?

☐ 20 pounds   ☐ 30 pounds   ☐ 10 pounds

5. The university that did the research is in which state?

☐ Michigan   ☐ Minnesota   ☐ Montana

Reading Comprehension

Name: _____

Main Idea: New Corn

I will clothe myself in spring clothing
And visit the slopes of the eastern hill.
By the mountain stream, a mist hovers,
Hovers a moment and then scatters.
Then comes a wind blowing from the south
That brushes the fields of new corn.

Directions: Answer these questions about the ancient poem called "New Corn" translated from the Chinese language.

1. The main idea is:

   The poet will dress comfortably and go to where the corn grows so he can enjoy the beauty of nature.

   The poet will dress comfortably and visit the slopes of the eastern hill, where he will plant corn.

2. From which direction does the wind blow?

   _____

3. Where does the mist hover?

   _____

4. What do you think the poet means by "spring clothing?"

   _____

Comprehension: The French Eat Differently

Many people believe that French people are very different from Americans. This is certainly true where eating habits are concerned! According to a report by the World Health Organization, each year the French people eat four times more butter than Americans. The French also eat twice as much cheese! In addition, they eat more vegetables, potatoes, grain and fish.

Yet, despite the fact that they eat **larger** amounts of these foods, the French take in about the same number of calories each day as Americans. (French and American men consume about 2,500 calories each day. French and American women take in about 1,600 calories daily.)

How can this be? If the French are eating more of certain types of foods, shouldn't this add up to more calories? And why are so few French people overweight compared to Americans? The answer: Americans consume **18 times** more refined sugar than the French, and drink twice as much whole milk!

Although many Americans believe the French wind up each meal with grand and gooey desserts, this just isn't so. Except for special occasions, dessert in a typical French home consists of fresh fruit or cheese. Many American families, on the other hand, like to end their meals with a bowl or two of ice cream or another sweet treat.

It's believed that this difference in the **kind** of calories consumed — rather than in the total **number** of calories taken in — is what causes many Americans to be chubby and most French people to be skinny.

Directions: Answer these questions about the eating habits of French and American people.

1. Name six types of foods the French people eat more of each year than Americans.

   _____

2. How many calories does the average French man eat each day? _____

3. How much whole milk does the average French person drink compared to the average American? _____

4. How much more refined sugar do Americans eat than the French?

   ☐ 2 times more   ☐ 18 times more   ☐ 15 times more

5. What do French families usually eat for dessert?

   ☐ French gooey   ☐ ice cream   ☐ fruit and cheese

Reading Comprehension

Recognizing Details: Chinese Cabbage

Many Americans enjoy Chinese food. In big cities, like New York and Chicago, many Chinese restaurants deliver their food in small boxes to homes. It's just like ordering a pizza! Then the people who ordered the "take-out" food simply open it, put it on their plates and eat it while it's hot.

Because it tastes so good, many people are curious about the ingredients in Chinese food. **Siu choy** and **choy sum** are two types Chinese cabbage that many people enjoy eating. **Siu choy** grows to be two- or three-feet around! Of course, it is chopped into small pieces before it is cooked and served. Its leaves are light green and soft. It is not crunchy like American cabbage. **Siu choy** is used in soups and stews. Sometimes it is pickled with vinegar and other ingredients and served as a side dish to other courses.

Choy sum looks and tastes different from **siu choy**. **Choy sum** grows to be only 8 to 10 inches long. It is a flowering cabbage that grows small yellow flowers. The flowers are "edible", which means they can be eaten. Its leaves are long and bright green. After its leaves are boiled for four minutes, **Choy sum** is often served as a salad. Oil and oyster sauce are mixed together and poured over **choy sum** as a salad dressing.

Directions: Answer the questions about Chinese cabbage.

1. Which Chinese cabbage grows small yellow flowers? _____

2. Which Chinese cabbage is served as a salad? _____

3. Is **siu choy** crunchy? _____

4. What ingredients are in the salad dressing used on **choy sum**?

   _____

5. What size does **siu choy** grow to be?

   _____

6. Name two main dishes **siu choy** is used in.

   _____

Reading Comprehension   Name: _____

Review

Here's a recipe for a special mashed potatoes treat that serves two people. The recipe is fast and easy to follow and the results are delicious!

Begin by peeling two large potatoes and cooking them in a pot of boiling water. When a fork or knife inserted into them pulls out easily, you will know they are done. Then take them from the pot and drain them well. Put them in a large mixing bowl and add 2 tablespoons of milk and 2 tablespoons of butter. Mash with a potato masher until the lumps are gone.

Then in a skillet, melt a tablespoon of butter and add 1 bunch of chopped green onions. Cook them about one minute. Add them to the potatoes and mix gently. Season with salt and pepper and add more butter if desired. Serve and eat!

Directions: Answer these questions about how to make mashed potatoes with green onions.

1. The main idea is:

    ____ This recipe, which has only 4 ingredients (plus salt and pepper) is fast and easy and the potatoes are delicious.

    ____ This recipe, which has only 5 ingredients (plus salt and pepper) is fast and easy, and the potatoes are delicious.

2. Name the main ingredients in this recipe (not including salt and pepper).

    _____

3. How many people does this recipe serve? _____

4. Number the following sequence of steps correctly.

    _____ Cook the chopped green onion for 1 minute.

    _____ Peel two potatoes.

    _____ Season with salt and pepper and serve.

    _____ Put the cooked potatoes in a bowl with milk and butter, then mash.

    _____ Add the onions to the mashed potatoes.

    _____ Boil the potatoes until they are done.

5. Give directions on what to do with the cooked potatoes after they are put in the bowl and before the green onions are added.

    _____